Tips & Guidance

When reading this book please remember the following key points;

- Reading should be a fun and pleasurable experience. Don't worry if your child does not want to read. Let them listen and allow your enthusiasm for the story attract their interest.

- Choose a time of day for reading and include this in your normal routine. For example after lunchtime or at bedtime. Most children benefit from a routine and look forward to story time.

- Encourage your child to read along with you based on their recall. It is very natural for children to do this.

- Allow your child to choose what they would like to read. Don't worry if they keep choosing the same book. Reading the same story over and over again helps them learn and should be encouraged. It is important to maintain your interest in the story as this will in turn hold your child's attention.

- Try to learn the Makaton Signs before you start to read with your child.

- Intonation and body language are an essential part of using Makaton Signs. Use eye contact and facial expressions as you are signing to provide essential meaning and context.

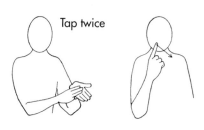

Mum   **said**

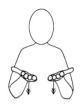   

Today   **we**   are   **going**   to   the   **shops**

Christmas Shopping
A Story Book With Makaton

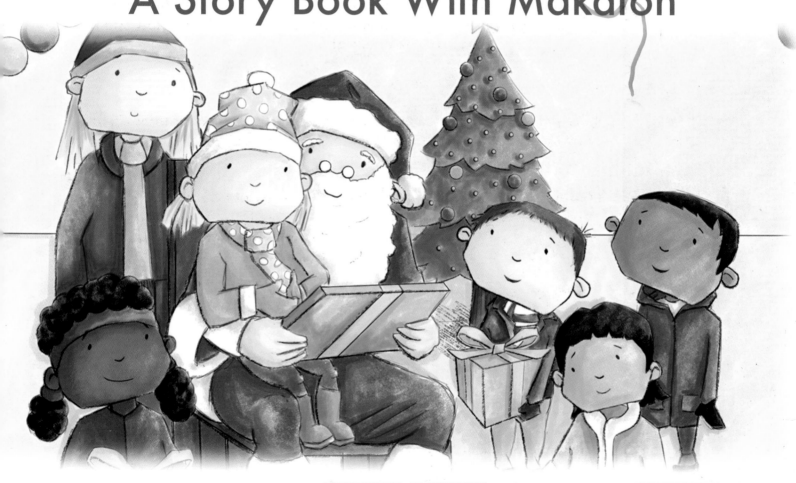

TIPI PUBLISHING LTD

Foreword

The following guidance is intended to help you enjoy reading with your child and benefit from using Makaton Signs.

If your child is new to reading you may find it helpful to begin with our 'My First Makaton' range of picture books. These simple books are designed to help your child become familiar with reading materials including how a book is held, and that pages are turned in sequence starting from the front cover moving towards the back.

The text throughout the story is accompanied by Makaton Signs. Using Makaton Signs when reading with your child helps them develop their communication skills, and follow the story.

Makaton Signs are always meant to be used with speech. The Makaton signs should be made while reading the story to your child.

Additional Makaton Signs are included towards the back of this book to help you discuss and explore the illustrations with your child.

The   **girl**   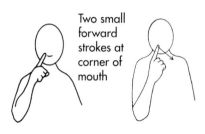 **said**

Two small
forward
strokes at
corner of
mouth

It's   **cold**

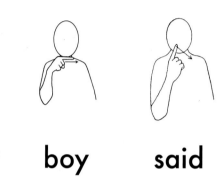

The **boy** **said**

There is our **bus**

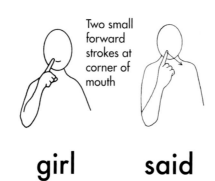

Two small forward strokes at corner of mouth

The **girl** **said**

Hands move with swirling movement down in front of body

It's **snowing**

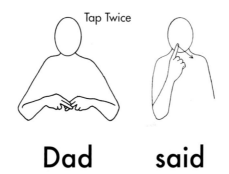

Tap Twice

Dad   **said**

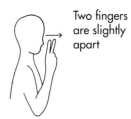

Two fingers
are slightly
apart

Whole
formation
circles twice

Look   at   these   great   **toys**

12

Tap twice

Mum   **said**

Stroke long beard

Mime holding sack over shoulder

Let's   **go**   and   **see**   Father   Christmas

14

Santa's Grotto

ENTER

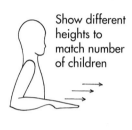
Show different heights to match number of children

Stroke long beard

Mime holding sack over shoulder

The **children** **said** **Father** **Christmas**

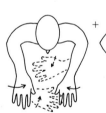
Mime wrapping parcel and tying string

gave US a **present**

16

17

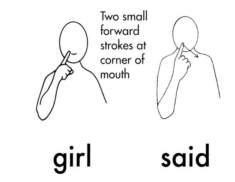

Two small forward strokes at corner of mouth

The **girl** **said**

Two fingers are slightly apart

Look at my **colouring** **pens**

18

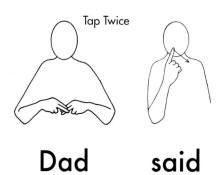

Dad   **said**

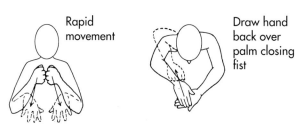

We've   **finished**   **shopping**

Tap twice

Mum **said**

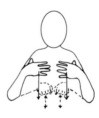

Put on your **pyjamas**

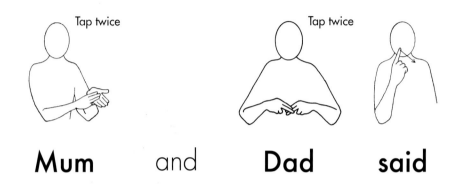

Mum   and   **Dad**   said

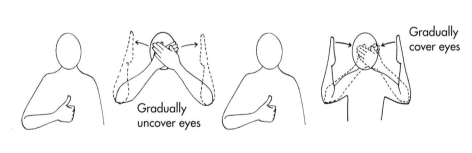

It's   been   a   **lovely**   **day**   **good**   **night**

24

Other Useful Signs

Tinsel

Index and middle fingers wiggle slightly

Turkey

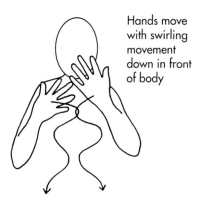

Hands move with swirling movement down in front of body

Snow

Happy/Merry

Other Useful Signs

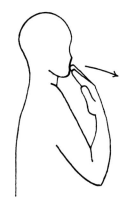

Thank you

Christmas Cracker

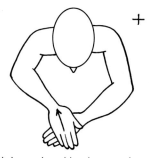

Slide top hand back towards body. Close and move back onto left hand

Christmas

Lights

Other Useful Signs

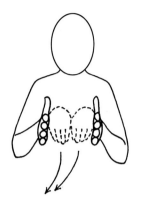

Sledge

Party

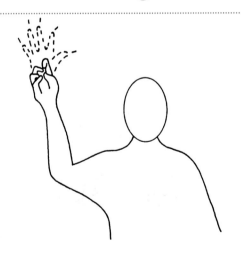

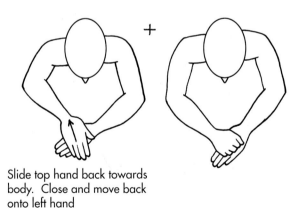

Slide top hand back towards body. Close and move back onto left hand

Star

Christmas

28

Other Useful Signs

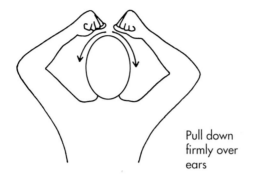

Pull down firmly over ears

Hat

As if smoothing glove over fingers. Repeat both hands

Gloves

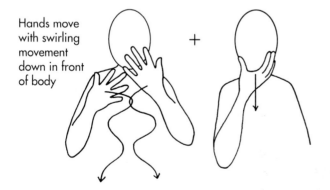

Hands move with swirling movement down in front of body

+

Snowman

Christmas Tree

Other books from Tipi Publishing Ltd

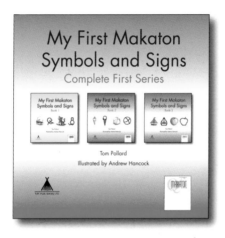

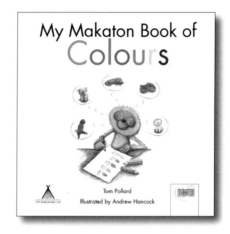

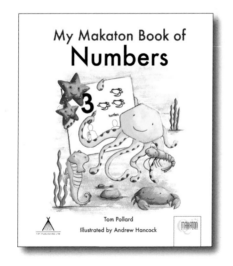

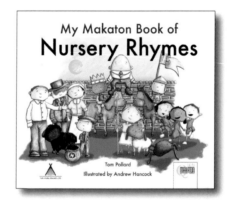

Other Makaton Titles

- My First Makaton Symbols & Signs Book 1 - ISBN - 9781907864094

- My First Makaton Symbols & Signs Book 2 - ISBN 9781907864100

- My First Makaton Symbols & Signs Book 3 - ISBN - 9781907864117

- My First Makaton Symbols & Signs - Complete Series - ISBN - 9781907864124

- My Makaton Books of Numbers - ISBN - 9781907864070

- My First Makaton Book of Colours - ISBN - 9781907864049

- My First Makaton Book of Nursery Rhymes ISBN - 9781907864131

- Going to the Park - A Story Book With Makaton - ISBN 9781907864155

- A Trip to the Seaside - A Story Book With Makaton - ISBN 9781907864162

- A Trip to the Zoo - A Story Book With Makaton - ISBN 9781907864179

- Days Out Complete Series - ISBN 9781907864156